CRAZY FACTS AND RECORDS

A whole lot of weird stuff for kids!

ARCTURUS

ARCTURUS

This edition published in 2010 by Arcturus Publishing Limited
26/27 Bickels Yard, 151–153 Bermondsey Street,
London SE1 3HA

ISBN: 978-1-84837-629-8
CH001573EN

Illustrations by Andy Peters
Design and Layout by Picnic

Printed in India

CONTENTS

 Totally Crazy   Keep your eyes peeled for these facts. They're so off the wall, they deserve a special mention!

 Don't try any of these crazy stunts at home, folks – you know it makes sense!

ANiMAL ANTiCS

The animal world is filled with all manner of weird and wonderful creatures. Many find a place in our home and end up pooping all over the carpet! But animals are capable of so much more than that. Read on and you'll find yourself wondering whether we humans really are the smartest critters on the planet.

Don't forget to check out ...

... the rats that like to surf **p8**

... the dogs that like to paint **p11**

... and the frog that likes to ride a motorbike! **p15**

Ninja Chimp

If he were still alive, martial arts expert Bruce Lee would have stiff competition from Charlie the Chimp.

Charlie, a 17-year-old chimpanzee, was awarded a black belt for his amazing display of karate skills in 1987. Today, he enjoys the high life – as well as touring the USA and showing off his technique, he appears on chat shows and in numerous adverts.

TIME TO CHILL
In between bouts of sparring, Charlie likes to relax by playing in his pool, reading magazines and feasting on tasty snacks.

STATS 'N' FACTS

Name: Charlie the Chimp
Weight: 90 kg/14.5 st
Owner: Carmen Presti
Home: Niagra Falls, USA
Fav food: Pizza, chicken wings
Fact: Charlie is far heavier than martial arts king, Bruce Lee.

GUESS WHAT?
Charlie has an arch rival in the shape of a 12-year-old monkey from Japan who can chop panels of wood in two with his bare hands!

Fashion Victims

While most countries like their guinea pigs playing in cages, the people of Peru prefer to dress them up.

Every year, in Huacho, Peru, the Festival of the Guinea Pig takes place. People flock to see these cute furry creatures dressed up as miners, peasants, kings and queens. Then they judge which one is the best dressed.

●●●●●●●●●●●●●●

Piggy Olympics

In 2006, 12 little piggies went to Moscow to compete in the third annual Pig Olympics.

Attracting entrants from seven different countries, including South Africa and the Ukraine, the special Olympics were made up of three events:

- A running race featuring obstacles and jumps
- A swimming event with pigs paddling across a pool
- A game where a ball pasted in fish oil (yuk!) was pushed around until a pig scored a goal

●●●●●●●●●●●●●●

Mighty Mouse House

It may not be a luxury penthouse but the humble tennis ball is keeping the harvest mouse alive.

Harvest mice were rapidly becoming Britain's no 1 snack for animal predators, so they started building nests in safer places above ground. Then wildlife experts stepped in and gave them a cosy tennis ball with a hole inside it to sleep in instead!

GUESS WHAT?
The balls used to shelter the harvest mice come from Wimbledon, the home of one of the world's greatest tennis tournaments.

NEST BUILDING
The tennis ball is attached to a pole above the ground. A hole is cut and a seed placed inside. The mouse climbs in to get the seed, then snoozes!

STATS 'N' FACTS

Name: Harvest mouse
Latin name: Micromys minutus
Home: Europe and Asia
Colour: Brown
Fact: Harvest mice are tiny – about the size of a coin.

Surf's Up, Ratty

They're best known for spreading the Bubonic Plague but did you know some rats are also surfboarding stars? Yes, really!

Fin and Tofu are two one-year-old rats who dazzle onlookers at the beach with their surfboarding tricks. They ride 1.2 m/4 ft waves and surf through 'tubes' (tunnels of water) for up to 20 minutes at a time. Thanks to their owner's training, these young rats fall off their boards less than most human surfers!

STATS 'N' FACTS

Names: Fin and Tofu
Home: Hawaii, USA
Owner: Boomer Hodel
Lifestyle: Beach bums
Fact: The rats own their own customised surfboards.

"Running on a wheel isn't enough for Fin and Tofu – they like a more extreme rush!"
Owner, Boomer Hodel

GUESS WHAT?
The surfing rodents are fed on a high protein, low carbohydrate diet to help keep them in tip-top shape for their antics on the waves.

Totally Crazy

Cat-astrophically Fat

Pussy lovers, think again. Put that tuna away!
It's time to meet some of the world's fattest cats.

• **Katy** is a noisy Siamese puss who lives in the Ural Mountains, Russia. Siamese cats are normally sleek and slender but not Katy. She weighs in at a whopping 22.5 kg/50 lbs – about the size of a six-year-old boy.

• Appropriately named, **Chubby**, belongs to Xu Jirong from China. His cat weighs 15 kg/33 lbs and has a waist size of 77 cm/30 in.

• Perhaps the most infamous fat cat was **Tiddles**, a stray adopted by a toilet attendant at Paddington Station, London, UK. Tiddles became a star and recieved fan mail as well as food from his fans.

GUESS WHAT?
There are no longer any official records kept for fat cats. This is to stop encouraging more people from overfeeding their pets.

GOBBLE IT UP
Katy's owner claims that her cat doesn't eat that much food. Mind you, she also claims that Katy can wolf down a hot dog in under a minute!

Salty Seafarer

Rats adore the water but none more so than one incredible rodent found off the coast of New Zealand.

In 2005, scientists radio-tagged a Norway rat for a study. However, it made a break for freedom and swam an amazing 400 m/1,312 ft in the sea before being recaptured. Some people reckon the intrepid swimmer may have set a new world record for a rat swimming in open water.

●●●●●●●●●●●●●●

Wheelie Lucky

Totally Crazy

You normally expect to see broken-down cars on the motorway but how about ... errr ... a hamster?

British motorists were amazed one day in 2006, when they spotted a hamster running along inside a plastic exercise ball on the M6 motorway. Roly, as he was nicknamed, was rescued by animal welfare workers. He was not prosecuted for driving without a licence!

●●●●●●●●●●●●●●

Doggy Masterpieces

The very idea might have had Van Gogh cutting his ear off in despair, but some dogs can actually paint.

The Shore Service Dogs in Britain are trained to help disabled people but they like doing a bit of artistic creation on the side. Their owner, Mary Stadelbach, says the dogs paint bright, abstract pictures. Their work fetches up to £230 per piece.

GUESS WHAT?
Stadelbacher doesn't claim that her dogs are the first to put paw to print, but she does believe they are the first to use an actual brush.

PAW PRINTS
Each dog-painted picture is signed with a black paw print by the canine artist responsible. So look closely the next time you see some art on a wall!

"Go paint, Sammy!"
calls Mary Stadelbach to her dogs during demonstrations

Smooching Pooches

If 356 dogs turn up to get married, it can't really be wrong!

In 2007, Littleton, Colorado, USA, a group of dog owners organised an arranged marriage for their canine pets. The big day saw the loved-up pooches swapping their collars for full wedding gear, and taking their 'bow-wow-vows'.

If a pet wedding like this takes your fancy, you can hire a wedding planner. They'll sort out:

• Perfect outfits – tuxedo, dress and veil
• A doggy marriage licence
• Wedding cake and canine treats

Price: US $1000 – we're not making this up!

"It was time to make it legal. Dezi is totally in love with Lucy."
Mother of dog, Lucy, one of the brides-to-be

GUESS WHAT?
The dog wedding in Littleton smashed the previous record held by the Netherlands. At the Dutch ceremony, only 54 loved-up pooches tied the knot.

Firefighters To The Rescue

What do you do if your hamster gets its head stuck between the bars of its cage?

It's obvious, of course. You call the fire brigade. That's exactly what the owner of a cute little hamster from Cheshire, UK, did when its head got wedged between the narrow metal bars of its cage. Luckily, in no time at all, the firefighters freed the furry critter and it lived to tell the tale.

●●●●●●●●●●●●●●●

Nuclear Kitty

Is it possible for a cat to grow grotesquely fat after being exposed to nuclear radiation?

Roger Degange shot to fame in 2001 when he claimed that his cat, Snowball, became obese because she had been wandering around a deserted nuclear facility. Sounds ridiculous? Well it is! The cruel prankster had just overfed her.

●●●●●●●●●●●●●●●

Pgymy Up Please

The world's officially smallest living monkey is a baby pygmy marmoset.

The tiny primate is a mere 35 cm/13.7 in tall when fully grown and weighs 100 g/3.5 oz. But beware, this animal isn't as cute a pet as it sounds. Expect a monkey to bite, scratch, cause damage and poop all over the house!

●●●●●●●●●●●●●●

Tall Tails

Summer is an American Paint Horse with a record-breaking tail. It's more than 3.81 m/12.5 ft long – about the length of a car.

Owner, Crystal Socha, keeps Summer's tail braided and covered in a tube sock when not showing her off. She combs and shampoos the tail every two months. It takes three hours at a time to complete this Herculean task because each hair is as fine as a fishing line.

●●●●●●●●●●●●●

Frog Of Many Talents

Performing frogs are something of a rarity unless you're Nong Oui from Thailand.

Able to sit on a toy motorbike and more than happy to be handled, Nong Oui, caused quite a splash when she was shown to reporters. But it was her talent for predicting the National Lottery Numbers that made her an even bigger froggy hit!

GUESS WHAT?

Locals examined the patterns on Nong Oui's skin to find their Lottery numbers. The amazing clairvoyant frog came up trumps 10 times in a row.

STATS 'N' FACTS

Name: Nong Oui
Type: Black-spotted frog
Home: Thailand
Hobbies: Riding toy vehicles
Fact: As well as Harley Davidson's, Nong Oui likes to ride dumpster trucks.

GROUNDED

Sadly, Nong Oui's owner had to ground her when the frog's run of luck ended and she stopped predicting the winning Lottery numbers.

Squirrels On The Water

To old people, Twiggy is the name of a mini-skirted model. To animal lovers, she's a waterskiing squirrel.

Twiggy is a squirrel from Florida, USA, who has been trained to waterski by the Best family since the late 1970s using a remote-controlled boat. She's a huge hit with the American public, having appeared on many chat shows, and she's even starred in hit Hollywood movies, including *Dodgeball* and *Anchorman*.

"Twiggy is really quite happy with her life. She has her own room at home with trees to climb."
Lou Ann Best, dismissing complaints from animal rights campaigners

MURKY SECRET
Twiggy, who has been waterskiing for over 30 years, is a series of squirrels who go by the same name. Squirrels only live for about six years.

Get A Pet-icure

Totally Crazy

If you want a set of perfect feet, then you'll need 5,000 flesh-eating fish to do the job.

When razors were banned for use in pedicures in the US state of Virginia, salon owner, Yvonne Le, scoured the Internet to find an alternative. She hit the jackpot when she discovered the garra fish – it loves nibbling away at dead skin! Customers have described the sensation as being like hundreds of delicate kisses.

● ● ● ● ● ● ● ● ● ● ● ● ● ●

My Teen Tiny Pony

Need the perfect pet to walk in the park? Try Thumbelina, the world's smallest living horse.

Thumbelina comes from a genuine miniature horse breed but she's also a dwarf too, which makes her extra-small and extra-special. She's only about 44 cm/17 in tall. Thumbelina is nicknamed 'Mini Mini' by her owners. They say she likes nothing better than bossing the bigger horses around!

● ● ● ● ● ● ● ● ● ● ● ● ● ●

You Calling Me Ugly?

Every year in Sonoma-Marin, California, USA, the world's ugliest dog competition takes place.

Dog owners from across the country travel to the contest to show off their pets' challenging looks. The 2008 winner was Gus, from Florida. Poor old Gus had just one eye after a fight with a tomcat and only three legs. Mind you, his owner loved him all the same!

● ● ● ● ● ● ● ● ● ● ● ● ● ●

Hamster Escapes
A Hammering

Cats are supposed to have nine lives but plucky Mike the Hamster from North Wales, UK, runs an extremely close second.

In 2006, Mike had an incredible escape from a shredder and three different kinds of crushing machine in an industrial waste unit. He was spun, shaken and nearly squashed to death before popping out at the other end unharmed after a four-minute destruction process. That's one lucky hamster!

● ● ● ● ● ● ● ● ● ● ● ● ● ●

Look Up That Tree!

Everyone knows that sure-footed goats are great at climbing mountains but a few also like to climb trees!

In southwest Morocco, the amazing local goats scale seriously high branches to feed on the delicious berries found in Argan trees. But that's not their only skill. They also help the local women to make Argan oil from the berries, which is used for cooking and beauty treatments.

Totally Crazy

GUESS WHAT?

Not all Argan oil is made from goat droppings. Modern machinery can make the oil directly from the berries. It's just not quite the same!

OIL RECIPE

Once the goats have eaten their fill, they poo out the kernels from the berry seed. Local women pick them up and grind them to make the Argan oil.

STATS 'N' FACTS

Local name: 'Ha-ha' goat
Latin name: Capra hircus
Home: Morocco
Colour: Black, white, brown
Fact: Some goats have been spotted balancing up to 9 m/ 30 ft high in the branches.

RIDICULOUS OBJECTS

Useless, oversized or bizarrely shaped – you can guarantee you'll find an everyday object that's been 'ridiculized'. For years, madcap inventors have been busy in their garden sheds dedicating their lives to developing alternatives to everyday items and making the world laugh.

Don't forget to check out ...

... the toilet with a grass seat **p24**

... the monster mobile guitar **p27**

... and the shopping trolley motorcycle! **p34**

Motoring Along

Sometimes a boring old car isn't enough, especially when you can have a one in the shape of a cricket bat!

India's Sudhakar Yadav is a man with a mission – he's built over 200 motorized vehicles in the shape of everything from footballs to hamburgers. All of them, including his barmy motorized cricket bat car, work. Check out more of his creations below:

• A two-seater Valentine's car adorned with hearts and roses for loved-up couples who want to take a ride

• A world-record-breaking tricycle that is a staggering 12.5 m/41 ft tall and took three years to build

GUESS WHAT?
You can see all of Sudhakar's vehicles in his museum in Hyderbad, India. The place is extremely popular, attracting up to 1,000 visitors a day.

STATS 'N' FACTS

Name: Cricket bat car
Top speed: 60 kmh/40 mph
Time to build: Six months
Cost: Approx £1,000
Fact: The cricket bat car was built to support India in the 2007 Cricket World Cup.

Rotating Fork

If you like spaghetti but have a hard time twirling it around your fork, then this is the invention for you.

Invented by Mr Kenji Kawakami (see page 24), the rotating spaghetti fork is ideal for lazy foodies everywhere. However, there is one major problem. Imagine the spaghetti wrapping automatically around the fork – great. Now imagine the pasta sauce flying everywhere – not so great!

● ● ● ● ● ● ● ● ● ● ● ● ●

Giant Board Game

A board game can get boring but not when it's a giant version of Monopoly with houses and hotels 1,700 times larger than their original size.

To play the whopping board game, head to Monopoly In The Park, San Jose, USA. The 86 sq m/926 sq ft board is officially the largest outdoor version of the game in the world. Expect to wear huge token-shaped hats and a prison outfit if you get sent to jail.

● ● ● ● ● ● ● ● ● ● ● ● ●

A Truck Load Of Art

Is it a work of art or just plain ridiculous? Make your own mind up about the crazy Big Rig Jig sculpture.

Created in 2007 by US artist Mike Ross for the Burning Man Festival, the sculpture featured two full-sized 18-wheeler tanker trucks, towering four storeys high. Behind the craziness, was a serious message about how the oil industry has a powerful hold over our global society. Make of it what you will!

GUESS WHAT?

Artist Ross created a smaller plastic model before beginning the full-sized piece, so he could be sure his monster-sized sculpture would work.

STATS 'N' FACTS

Name: Big Rig Jig
What: Giant sculpture
Where: Nevada Desert, USA
Why: For The Burning Man experimental art festival
Fact: Every year, a giant wooden effigy is burnt at the festival.

"... it should give you a sense of danger and fear, and that something is wrong."
Artist Mike Ross talking about his towering tanker sculpture

The Art Of Chindogu

When is an invention useless but also useful?
Welcome to the Japanese art of Chindogu!

Mr Kenji Kawakami is the creator of Chindogu, which
loosely translated means 'un-useless ideas'. He has
invented hundreds of absurd items that have become
strangely popular. Check these ones out:

- An outdoor toilet seat with artificial
  grass to keep your bottom warm

- A two-way sandal with toes at both
  ends so you can wear it both ways

- An alarm clock with sharp pins on the off-button
  that prick you when you try to turn it off

"People need to laugh for no reason
... the concept is: you have it, I have it,
everybody has this wackiness."
Kenji Kawakami explains why he
continues with Chindogu

GUESS WHAT?
There is method behind
the inventor's madness.
He believes that his
ideas could make us
question our views on
consumerism.

24

Tour de Farce

Next time the Tour De France hits town, keep your eyes peeled for a red devil towing a giant bicycle.

German-born Dieter 'Didi' Senft can regularly be found following the famous Tour de France cycling competition dressed up as the devil. El Diablo, as he is known, has been cheering on the riders for years, and paints a devil's pitch fork on the road several hours beforehand to announce his arrival.

• • • • • • • • • • • • • •

Potty Car

A toilet-shaped car is the way to go if you want to make a splash!

Featuring a 50 cc engine and boasting a top speed of 40 kmh/25 mph, this crazy car will definitely get you noticed. The driver sits in the bowl with the lid up and zooms ... err ... pootles along. Thankfully, the toilet shape is an arresting design feature only – you aren't actually meant to poop in the toilet car as well!

• • • • • • • • • • • • • •

Hay Fever Hat

It's not attractive and you'll get funny looks in the street but your nose will thank you for wearing this hat.

Japanese inventor, Kenji Kawakami (see page 24) has created a bizarre hat for hay fever sufferers or indeed anyone who has the sniffles. Just reach up, unroll your toilet roll ... err, tissue ... and blow your nose. You'll never be caught with dangling bogeys again!

●●●●●●●●●●●●●●●

Topsy Turvy Houses

There are several upside-down houses around the world with their roofs stuck in the ground, but only a few have their interiors upside down too.

Pay a trip to the German island of Usedom and you'll discover a house that you enter through the attic. Inside, chairs, tables and carpets are upside down. Even the toilets are topsy turvy, so don't think of going. The house is part of a project called 'The World on its Head'. Other brain-straining exhibits are planned.

●●●●●●●●●●●●●●

Barmy Bikes

When not dressed up as the devil German 'Didi' Senft indulges his ot building bizarre bicycles.

'Didi' has built over 120 bonkers bicyc multiple word records. One of his lates inventions is the world's biggest mobile guitar. To peddle it, Didi lies flat on his back beneath a stonking half tonne of metal.

His other crazy creations include a World Cup tricycle featuring 100 footballs incorporated into its design.

STATS 'N' FACTS

Name: Mobile guitar
Length: 40 m/131 ft
Height: 4.2 m/13.8 ft
Fact: More than 300 m/980 ft of aluminium piping was used to build the mobile guitar.

GUESS WHAT?
Although Didi has ridden his giant guitar bike around a field, he's not allowed to take it on a public highway due to its incredible length.

...g A Splash

...fancy a swim, head off to the South American ...each resort of San Alfonso del Mar but make sure you pack some armbands in your suitcase.

The swimming pool at this resort is the longest in the world. It took five years to build and features a deep end taller than a three-bedroomed house. To cover one single length, you're in for a 1 km/0.5 mile doggy paddle but don't worry, if you can't face the distance, you can always jump in a kayak to take you across.

● ● ● ● ● ● ● ● ● ● ● ● ● ●

Shouting Vase

Totally Crazy

Feeling angry? Want to vent some frustration? Then give the shouting vase a go.

Aware that screaming loudly to relieve tension might scare everyone, Kenji Kawakami (see page 24) has thoughtfully invented the shouting vase. Simply put it to your lips and shout into the opening at the top. The vase muffles the outcry into a whisper, thanks to its soundproofed insides. Genius!

● ● ● ● ● ● ● ● ● ● ● ● ●

Teeny Tiny Hard Drive

Computer hard drives are shrinking but Toshiba have one that is small enough to sit on your finger!

Back in 2004, electronics giant Toshiba unveiled the world's smallest hard drive. It weighed a meagre 2 g/0.004 lb. In 2007, the company boosted the memory from 4 to 8 GB. The hard drive has already been put to good use in a mobile phone released in Japan.

●●●●●●●●●●●●●●

Board Game Madness

Think that a game of Monopoly can be a drag sometimes, well how about playing for 70 hours non-stop? That's the world record for the longest game of Monopoly ever.

Other crazy board game world records include:

• Playing them in the bath for 99 hours
• Playing them in a treehouse for 286 hours
• Playing them while upside for 26 hours

●●●●●●●●●●●●●●

Wheelie Weird

The next time you're in Michigan, USA, keep your eyes peeled for Kerry McLean sitting inside a giant rubber tyre – a monowheel – motoring along!

Although first proposed in the 19th century as a serious means of transport, today the monowheel is a cult object. McLean has created a top-of-the-range vehicle, known as the Rocket Roadster, which reaches a staggering speed of 86 kmh/56 mph.

"It's not easy to ride ... it's like riding a wheelie the whole time."
Mark Cernicky, another monowheel expert from Cycleworld magazine

ROCKET RECORD
McLean has spent years riding monowheels. With his Rocket Roadster, he set the world land speed record for powered single wheelers.

GUESS WHAT?
If you want to indulge a passion for riding monowheels, you can. McLean's vehicles are fully road legal and available to buy.

Living in a Toilet

When house prices go down the toilet, a toilet-shaped house is the best you can ask for.

Made from steel, glass and white concrete, the toilet house has two bedrooms, two guest rooms and ... yes, you've guessed it ... four deluxe toilets. Some of the toilets even have motion sensors to lift the lid automatically when they detect your behind.

"The toilet house has become a new cultural icon in the toilet culture movment."
Statement from the World Toilet Association

RENT IT
You can rent the toilet house for US $50,000 a day. The money isn't wasted – it's used to aid developing countries.

STATS 'N' FACTS

What: Toilet-shaped house
Name: Haewoojae
Where: South Korea
Floor space: 419 sq m/4,510 sq ft
Fact: This architectural marvel was built in 2007 for the World Toilet Association.

GUESS WHAT?

The toilet house was built by Sim Jae Duck. He is known as Mr Toilet because of his work trying to turn public restrooms into pleasant places.

16,000 For Dinner

In 1998, in Lisbon, Portugal, a huge table was set across the Vasco da Gama bridge for 16,000 hungry diners.

Stretching for 5 km/3 miles and spanning one-third of the length of the bridge, it became the longest dining table ever laid. Guests enjoyed a traditional Portuguese dish, the famous Feijoada stew ... all 10 tonnes of it.

● ● ● ● ● ● ● ● ● ● ● ● ● ●

Pass Me The Butterstick

Fed up of using a knife to butter your toast? Well, try the no-fuss butterstick instead.

Totally Crazy

Glue meets butter in this silly but smart idea that saves on the washing up. Dispensed in a glue-applicator-style stick, you just rub the butter directly on your toast, then replace the lid. It's the ultimate in laziness. The inventor? Of course, it's the irrepressible Mr Kenji Kawakami, the master of Chindogu (see page 24).

● ● ● ● ● ● ● ● ● ● ● ● ● ●

Nano Book

You're guaranteed to get serious eye strain with the world's smallest ever book.

The size of a match head and tiny enough to sit on the end of your finger, the world's smallest commercially produced book was introduced to the world in 2002 by a German publishing company. To avoid losing it in the post (or your pocket), the leatherbound mini-title is delivered in a mahogany box.

ZOOMING IN
To read the contents of the teeny book, the publisher has thoughtfully included a magnifying glass as part of the whole package.

GUESS WHAT?
There is a smaller book in existence. *Teeny Ted from Turnip Town,* a one-off children's book is so tiny you need a microscope to see it!

STATS 'N' STUFF

What: World's smallest book
Size: 2.4 x 2.9 mm/0.09 x 0.11 in
Number of pages: 26
Cost: US $1,000
Fact: There is no plot to this bonsai book. Each page contains a single letter of the alphabet.

"It was printed in the usual way but all the machinery and tools had to be created in miniature first."
Publisher, Alexander Nedo

Off His Trolley

When is a shopping trolley not a shopping trolley? When it's a motorbike!

Boasting a 50 cc engine and travelling up to 45 kmh/28 mph, Duncan Everson has built a mental motorbike out of a metal shopping cart. The motorized masterpiece is totally road legal and Duncan can be seen regularly whizzing past the supermarket in Palmerston North, on the North Island of New Zealand.

DO IT YOURSELF
To create his trolley transport, Everson attached a moped engine to the metal shopping cart and then fitted wheels from a lawnmower.

"I take it out and cruise round The Square on Friday and Saturday nights. I get a few looks!"
Duncan Everson on his shopping trolley riding habit

GUESS WHAT?
The New Zealand police regularly pull over Everson when he's out on the road to check that his motorized trolley really is roadworthy.

Lego Of Me

Have you ever tried to build a Lego tower? What about one that needs the help of an outdoor crane?

After four days, using 500,000 lego bricks, the folks at Legoland in Windsor, UK, managed to create the world's tallest Lego tower at 29.3 m/96.1 ft. Congratulations all round. However, just months later, another group in Vienna, Austria, broke the world record with just a handful more bricks.

● ● ● ● ● ● ● ● ● ● ● ● ●

Giant Toilet Roll

In 2007, London, UK, the world's longest toilet roll was unrolled from the world's largest toilet roll holder.

The unravelled toilet paper stretched a ridiculous 18.3 km/11.4 miles. Even though it was created for an outdoor publicity stunt, the toilet roll could actually be used because it was made by a leading toilet roll manufacturer – let's just hope no one did!

● ● ● ● ● ● ● ● ● ● ● ● ●

EXTREME RiSKS

We all like to do things that give us a buzz, like riding a rollercoaster or being driven in a super-fast car. But for some folks, such pastimes are nowhere near enough. Take a look at a bunch of people who spend their lives searching for the ultimate adrenalin rush.

Don't forget to check out ...

... the wheelchair skateboarder who performs backflips **p41**

... the people who 'flew' across the sea in an inflatable kangaroo **p43**

... and the rally driver who takes his car snowboarding! **p51**

To Infinity And Beyond

Look up into the skies and there's a faint chance you'll see a man strapped to a plane wing without the plane!

It may sound like something out of a James Bond film but this is for real. Yves Rossy broke the world record for being the first person to fly solo across the English Channel strapped to a jet-propelled wing. He made the 35.4 km/22 mile flight in 9 minutes and 7 seconds, travelling at an average speed of 200 kmh/124 mph.

GUESS WHAT?

Rossy used to fly Mirage fighters for the Swiss army and is now an airline pilot. In his spare time, he enjoys parachute jumping. What a surprise!

"I fuse with my machine. It was my dream as a boy to be a bird."
Yves Rossy explaining his passion for flying

WHAT NEXT?

It is thought that Yves Rossy's next daredevil jet-powered challenge will be to fly solo through the Grand Canyon in the USA.

STATS 'N' FACTS

Who: Yves Rossy
Famous for: Flying strapped to a jet-propelled plane wing
Fact: Yves built his world-record-breaking four jet engine himself in his garage.

Fireball Bus

Flying through the air for 33 m/108 ft over 15 motorbikes in a burning bus isn't for everyone, but Steve Hudis certainly likes it.

Hollywood stuntman, Hudis, pulled off this spectacular fireball feat in 2008. In the process, he inadvertently broke a world record the longest jump ever by a bus.

● ● ● ● ● ● ● ● ● ● ● ● ● ●

Lion King

Lions have big pointy teeth and are known for biting and eating people, so you'd think lions and children wouldn't mix - wrong!

Jorge Elich, an eight-year-old boy has become the world's youngest lion tamer. He is such an expert that he now practises his deadly art at the Circus Paris in El Ejido, Spain. His gift for staring into the jaws of death is not new – he actually started taming lions when he was just five years old.

● ● ● ● ● ● ● ● ● ● ● ● ● ●

The Human Spider

Meet the human spider who climbs up the sides of skyscrapers with no safety equipment at all.

Alain 'Spiderman' Roberts, has been climbing without ropes since he was a child. His first achievement was scaling eight floors up to his parent's flat because he had forgotten his keys when he was 12. Since then he has earned a world record for the most extreme solo ascent up the Gorge of Verdon in France.

"A city is like a range of mountains with one little difference – there will always be new skyscrapers under construction."
Death-defying climber, Alain Roberts

SKY HIGH
The human spider has managed to climb over 70 famous buildings including the Eiffel Tower in France and the Empire State Building in the USA.

GUESS WHAT?
Alain was arrested for climbing the One Houston Centre in Texas, USA, without authorisation. He was only 2 m/6.5 ft off the ground.

Wacky Wild Air Race

The Red Bull Air Race World Championships is certainly not for the faint-hearted.

The Championship showcases the world's best pilots who race against the clock around an aerial race track marked out by inflatable pylons. They twist and turn approximately 4.5 m/15 ft from the ground at breakneck speeds of 320 kmh/198 mph. The reward? Nothing – just knowing you're the best!

GUESS WHAT?

Planes can safely slice through the pylons marking the course and continue on their way. They are designed to be as safe as possible.

CITY TO CITY

The six venues chosen for each round of the 2009 air race were Abu Dhabi, San Diego, Windsor (Canada), Budapest, Porto and Barcelona.

STATS 'N' FACTS

What: Red Bull Air Race
Where: Six different cities
Race track length: 5 km/3 miles
Fact: If the pilots clip one of the air pylons with their wings, they receive a 10-second penalty.

Wheel Deal

'Hardcore sitting' is the appropriate label Aaron 'Wheels' Fotherington has given to the extreme stunts he likes to pull in his wheelchair at a US skatepark.

Teenage Fotherington pulls the kinds of feats and tricks that would leave a pro-skateboarder looking tame, and is so good that he has landed himself a world record for performing the first ever backflip in a wheelchair.

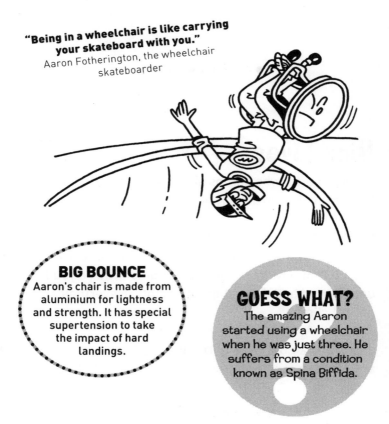

"Being in a wheelchair is like carrying your skateboard with you."
Aaron Fotherington, the wheelchair skateboarder

BIG BOUNCE
Aaron's chair is made from aluminium for lightness and strength. It has special supertension to take the impact of hard landings.

GUESS WHAT?
The amazing Aaron started using a wheelchair when he was just three. He suffers from a condition known as Spina Biffida.

Horrendous Hobbies

Totally Crazy

Brit Thomas Blackthorn is a man of many bizarre hobbies including eating glass, swallowing razor blades and sleeping in a pit of snakes.

Perhaps his most spectacular feat was pushing a giant demolition hammer down his throat and holding it there with no hands for three seconds. When you know the hammer weighed 38 kg/84 lbs – about half the weight of a grown man – you realise that this was no mean feat!

● ● ● ● ● ● ● ● ● ● ● ● ●

Nine Lives

Alain Roberts, who climbs skyscrapers for fun (see page 39), has had several lucky escapes from near-death.

In 1982, he fell 15 m/49 ft head-first and was in a five-day coma with multiple fractures. Alain recovered but it left him with vertigo, the condition where you feel unbalanced and dizzy at great heights. Nevertheless, he still climbs.

Just a quick note folks to remind you again not to try any of these stunts yourself. Even the experts fail!

● ● ● ● ● ● ● ● ● ● ● ●

Dangerous Sports Club

You may have seen crazy guys on TV pulling risky stunts but their antics are nothing compared to those of the Dangerous Sports Club.

The UK club was started in the late 1970s by David Kirke, and quickly gained risk-loving recruits. Check out just a few of their insane feats below:

• The world's first ever modern bungee jump

• Fying across the English Channel tucked into the pouch of an inflatable kangaroo

"A jumbo pilot saw me at 100 ft and assumed it was a UFO."
David Kirke on crossing the English Channel in his helium-filled kangaroo

GUESS WHAT?
Perhaps the club's finest achievement was when Alan Weston flew around the Houses of Parliament in a gorilla outfit playing the saxophone!

ON THE CHASE
Weston was chased by a police helicopter in his gorilla outfit before being picked up. His day job now? A rocket scientist for the US airforce.

Head Over Heels

In August 2006, Travis Pastrana managed to perform the world's first freestyle motocross double backflip on his bike at the fearsome X Games.

The amazing 720 degree flip landed him the highest score ever given by the judges at the Best Trick event. Not surprising when you consider how dangerous the stunt was – landing wrongly could have, at best, destroyed his career and, at worst, killed him.

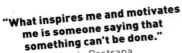

"What inspires me and motivates me is someone saying that something can't be done."
Travis Pastrana

GUESS WHAT?
Travis has stated that he will not be attempting another double backflip. He reckons it's up to others to follow in his tyre marks.

FEEL THE FEAR
Travis wasn't sure whether to go ahead with his stunt up until the last minute – he let a game of 'rock, paper, scissors', decide for him!

Buried Alive

Being buried alive in a wooden box is one way of passing the time, but surely it's not the best.

Well, Geoff Smith from Mansfield, UK, might disagree. He was buried alive for nearly five months in a box 1.8 m/6.8 ft long under the garden of his local pub. For company, Geoff had a small TV, personal stereo, mobile phone and mini Christmas tree. Yes, he even spent Christmas underground!

"... for the last 30 years, it's been his ambition to go and bury himself in a box."
Hartley Hughes, pub landlord

STATS 'N' FACTS

Who: Geoff Smith
Famous for: Being buried alive
How long: 147 days
How deep: 1.8 m/5.9 ft
Fact: Geoff breathed through a tube which was also used to pass food down to him.

TIMELY TRIBUTE
Geoff buried himself alive in tribute to his late mother, who clearly wasn't claustrophic either. In 1968, she set the original world record of 110 days.

GUESS WHAT?
The record for being buried alive without food or water belongs to Zdenek Zahradka from the Czech Republic who spent 10 days in a coffin.

When Risks Go Wrong

The Dangerous Sports Club (see page 43) have had many successes but some of their feats do go wrong.

In 2000, Stella Young was launched 21 m/69 ft into the air from a giant catapult. She travelled at 80 kmh/ 50 mph before coming back down to earth. When she hit the safety net, she bounced out and broke her pelvis. Luckily, plucky Stella made a speedy recovery.

● ● ● ● ● ● ● ● ● ● ● ● ● ●

Human Fireball

Not many people like the idea of being flame-grilled but it doesn't bother stuntman and daredevil Ted Batchelor.

Ted's favourite trick is to set himself on fire, walk around, then throw himself off a waterfall to put out the flames. The US human fireball first tried the stunt in 1976 for a bet and has repeated it many times since.

Ted has been burnt several times in his career and what he does is full of danger. Don't try this at home!

● ● ● ● ● ● ● ● ● ● ● ● ● ●

Ride The Monster

How do you fancy surfing a tidal bore wave on a river? Sounds easy? Well, think again.

Tidal bores are turbulent waves that travel inland against the current. They sweep down rivers at speeds of up to 40 kmh/25 mph. The longest non-stop tidal bore surfing record was set by Brazilian Serginho Laus. He stayed on his board for an incredible 33 minutes and 15 seconds, travelling 10.1 km/6.3 miles.

"The wave is very powerful and can destroy anything – trees, local houses, islands."
Serginho Laus on the power of tidal bore waves

WILD WAVES
Tidal bores are known as 'pororocas' in Brazil. This translates as 'monster' or 'murderer'. The locals know how unpredictable these waves are.

GUESS WHAT?
The Qiantang River in China has the most notorious tidal bore in the world. The longest anyone has managed to surf it is a mere 11 seconds.

STATS 'N' STUFF

Who: Serginho Laus
Famous for: Surfing tidal bores
Where: Arguari River, Brazil
Fact: Some tidal bore waves measure up to 9 m/25 ft high and travel up to 300 km/186 miles.

Snow No Fear

Riding a bike down a snow-covered mountain is not recommended, but it will make the bike go very fast!

That's exactly what Austrian Markus Stoeckl did to smash the world speed record for series mountain bikes when he careered down a 45 degree icy mountain slope in Chile for 2000 m/6,560 ft. The high-speed run took him 40 seconds to complete, travelling at a staggering 338.7 kmh/210.4 mph.

"I was very calm. At the end of the course, I had the feeling that I was watching myself riding."
Markus Stoeckl on breaking his mountain biking world record

IT'S STEAMY!
Markus had to hold his breath for the ride. This was to stop the warmth of his breath steaming up the aerodynamic helmet he was wearing.

GUESS WHAT?
Markus beat the previous eight-year-old world record by 22.5 kmh/ 14 mph. Guess who set that record? He did, of course!

Crazy Bull Run

If you find yourself on the streets of Pamplona, Spain, between 7–14 July at 8 am, you might want to hide.

This is when the extremely dangerous tradition of the running of the bulls takes place. People dressed in white with red neckerchiefs try to outrun six bulls and two herds of bullocks along an 825 m/2,706 ft course. It takes only three minutes to complete but the chances of being trampled or speared in the chest are high.

●●●●●●●●●●●●●●

Tongue Lift

Thomas Blackthorn, the man with the iron throat (see page 42) also has a spectacular tongue.

In July 2007, he set a world record for the heaviest tongue lift by hoisting up a stonking 12 kg/26 lbs of pasta in a glass-walled box. Now all you geeks out there, go and check the weight of one packet to get an idea of how much pasta that really is!

●●●●●●●●●●●●●●

Stunt Junkie

Travis Pastrana, the motocross backflip hero (see page 44) also enjoys skydiving.

Not so extreme? But he likes to do it without a parachute! In September 2008, the adrenalin junkie leapt from a plane at 3,810 m/12,500 ft minus his essential package. He then glided his way to his jump partner's back and climbed on before his fellow skydiver opened the one parachute between them.

●●●●●●●●●●●●●●

Full Body Burn

Human fireball Ted Batchelor doesn't just set himself alight (see page 46), he breaks world records at the same time too.

In 2004, Ted set the record for the longest full-body burn without an oxygen supply. He managed to stay alight (and alive) for 2 minutes and 38 seconds.

●●●●●●●●●●●●●●

Shocked By The Block

What do you do when being a succesful rally driver isn't enough? Well, you could try car jumping stunts instead.

In his spare time, rally driver Ken Block loves to go jumping in state-of the-art cars just for kicks. His most incredible achievement was in 2007 at the New Zealand Snow Park. He pulled off one of the most amazing feats ever by making a huge 21 m/68 ft jump in sync with a pro-snowboarder. Cool or what?!

Totally Crazy

"I know the physics: 90 miles per hour through trees sideways is pretty damn scary."
Ken Block on the danger involved in performing his snow stunt

STATS 'N' FACTS

Who: Ken Block
Famous for: Car jump stunts
Stunt vehicle: A Subaru Impressa WRX STi
Fact: Ken is also the co-founder of a successful shoe business.

GUESS WHAT?
Ken attempted another jump which was less successful. He overshot the landing ramp and landed his car nose-first in the ground.

INCREDIBLE PEOPLE

Some people are born a bit different while others spend a lifetime trying to get themselves noticed. Whatever the case, the world is full of peculiar but incredible people. This section is dedicated to these fearless folk and their amazing attributes.

Don't forget to check out ...

... the hairy family with a talent for acrobatics **p57**

... the men with the weirdest beards **p62**

... and the crazy Frenchman who ate an aeroplane! **p65**

Human Pincushion

Brazilian-born Elaine Davidson is the current world record holder for being the most pierced woman on the planet.

The former nurse, who now lives in Edinburgh, Scotland, was first spotted when she had 462 piercings. Today, she has more than 4,000. Elaine has calculated that all her metal studs and rings together weigh a whopping 3 kg/6.6 lbs – that's like carrying around two whole chickens all the time.

"People often just want to look at me or touch me – some even want to kiss me!"
Elaine explains people's reactions to her piercings

METAL FOR LIFE
Elaine never takes her piercings out. She even goes to bed wearing them. They don't bother her at all and she sleeps soundly every night.

STATS 'N' FACTS

Who: Elaine Davidson
Famous for: Covering her body with metal piercings
Fact: 192 of Elaine's piercings are on her face. It is completely covered with studs and rings!

GUESS WHAT?

Elaine loves extremes of all kind – she enjoys walking on fire, sleeping on a bed of nails and has earned herself a black belt in judo in Japan.

Eyes-A-Poppin'

Totally Crazy

Please don't try this at home but there are people who can pop their eyeballs almost out of their eye sockets.

American Kim Goodman is one such 'eye popper'. In 2007, her eyes were measured protruding 12 mm/ 0.47 in out from her face, making her look like a crazy cartoon character. Popping your eyeballs strains the blood vessels and nerves that attach your eyes to your head, so we suggest you leave it to the experts.

• • • • • • • • • • • • • • •

Corset Queen

American Cathie Jung has the world's smallest waist, measuring a teeny 38.1 cm/15 in.

To achieve it, Cathie has not gone under the knife. Instead she has worn corsets pulled tightly day and night for over 25 years. Cathie's husband, an orthopaedic surgeon, believes her corset-wearing does no harm and could help to support her spine rather than damage it.

• • • • • • • • • • • • • •

Bendy Skater Boy

Meet Aniket Chindak, the amazing seven-year-old from India who does the splits on roller skates, then whizzes under parked cars.

Aniket holds the unofficial world record for limbo-skating under the most cars in a row. His total is 57 vehicles in 45 seconds. He is currently in training to set a new official world record of 100 cars in 60 seconds, so watch this space!

TOP TECHNIQUE
The trick to skating under so many cars at once is to travel fast enough before bending down into the splits at the last moment.

GUESS WHAT?
Aniket trains for up to four hours a day. In a single week, he may travel as much as 97 km/ 60 miles on his roller skates!

STATS 'N' FACTS

Who: Aniket Chindak
Famous for: Limbo-skating under rows of cars
Fact: When Aniket is skating, his body is never more that 20 cm/ 8 in above the ground.

Speed Piercing

Imagine having 1,015 body piercings in one go.

That's exactly what Kam Ma did in April 2006 when he and UK-based Charlie Wilson (the piercer) set the world record for the most piercings in a single session. The whole process took 7 hours and 55 minutes. That's a very long time to say 'oooooouuuuuch'!

● ● ● ● ● ● ● ● ● ● ● ● ● ●

ice Man

How do you fancy climbing freezing Mount Everest in nothing but your undies?

Well, Wim Hof from Holland doesn't seem to mind. Ice Man, Wim, can withstand temperatures that would prove fatal to the rest of us. He reckons this is due to 'Tummo', a form of meditation he practises which allows him to generate heat in any part of his body. Check out his other icy feats:

• Chilling in a container of ice for over one hour
• Running a half marathon barefoot in the Arctic

● ● ● ● ● ● ● ● ● ● ● ● ● ●

Hair-raising Family

The Gomez family is a remarkable one. Many family members suffer from a condition which gives them thick hair all over their bodies including their faces.

Due to their condition, they had a tough start in life, spending their childhood as part of a sideshow sat in a cage where they were known as the 'wolf children'.

Fortunately, they were rescued by the son of a circus owner and eventually trained in the performing arts.

GUESS WHAT?

There are about 20 Gomez family members who have the genetic condition that gives them overly hairy bodies. It's known as hypertrichosis.

ACROBATICS

Today, brothers Danny and Larry Ramos Gomez perform as acrobats for the Mexican National Circus where they can show off their skills.

"I'd never take it off. I am very proud to be who I am."
Larry Ramos Gomez talking about the hair on his body

Super Strength

If you're looking for a pair of rippling biceps, then Georges Christen is your man.

Frenchman George is so strong that he doesn't always know his own strength. Once while admiring a car at a motor show, he accidently managed to break off the bumper! However, we can assure you that the feats of strength below were all planned.

- Ripping up 23 telephone directories in two minutes
- Bending 269 nails in one hour
- Carrying a woman perched on a table in his teeth for 10 m/32 ft

"I wanted to be that person the kids were amazed at."
George Christen explains why he carries out his crazy feats of super strength

DEEP BREATH
George enjoys blowing up empty hot water bottles too for a laugh. It takes him a meagre 40 seconds to inflate one before it explodes!

GUESS WHAT?
Claiming to have set over 20 world records, George regularly tours the world with his PowerShow display. It's a treat not to be missed.

Tall Story

Bao Xishun never has to worry about reaching the top shelf in the supermarket. That's because he's the world's tallest man.

Life hasn't always been easy though for the gentle giant. He's in good health, but for many years he found it hard to find love. However in 2007, he finally tied the knot with a woman from his home town. They are now the proud parents of an average-sized baby boy!

GUESS WHAT?
In 2006, Bao saved two dolphins. They had swallowed plastic, which he was able to remove from their stomachs with his extra-long arms.

STATS 'N' FACTS

Who: Bao Xishun
Famous for: World's tallest man
Home: Mongolia
Height: 2.3 m/7 ft 9 in
Fact: Bao is naturally tall. It's not due to a medical condition.

Mr Muscle

You would have thought that Australian Ray Moon would want to take it easy at the ripe old age of 79. But no – he's a championship body builder.

For the last four years, Ray's been working out for two and half hours up to six days a week. This led to him winning the over-60s division of the Body Building Championships in Melbourne, and he is now believed to be the oldest body builder on the planet.

●●●●●●●●●●●●●●●

Tree Man

It began with a single small wart on Dede Koswara's leg and ended with his feet and hands being covered in so many warts that his limbs looked like tree bark.

Dede, from Indonesia, suffers from a condition that stops his body from fighting off the warts. However, since being diagnosed, surgeons have performed four operations to help treat him. Thanks to these, Dede has been able to use his hands again for the first time in 10 years.

●●●●●●●●●●●●●●●

Plane Mad

Super strong Georges Christen (see page 58) has performed one feat that tops them all.

In 1990, he managed to stop three Cessna aircraft from taking off even though they were cranked up to full power. How? He used his arms to stop two of them from moving and his teeth to hold back the third one!

●●●●●●●●●●●●●●

Wee Man

He's the size of a six-month-old baby but 20-year-old He Ping Ping from Mongolia makes a big impression on everyone he meets.

He is 73 cm/2 ft 5 in tall, which makes him the world's shortest 'mobile' man (able to walk). Since being discovered, he has become an international jetsetter.

He Ping Ping has primordial dwarfism. When he was born, he was so tiny that he could fit into the palm of his father's hand.

●●●●●●●●●●●●●●

Weirdy Beardies

Totally Crazy

German Willi Chevalier is just one of a whole bunch of people who love to show off their facial whiskers.

Once every two years, owners of fine facial fur meet for a beard-off at the World Beard and Moustache Championships. In 2007, 252 competitors hit the UK to battle it out in the Moustache, Partial Beard and Full Beard categories. In each category, there were more classes including Musketeer and Partial Beard Freestyle which Willi won.

TOO FREAKY

One competitor in Berlin in 2005 used his beard to recreate the city's famous landmark, the Brandenburg Gate, and included horses and flags!

STATS 'N' FACTS

Who: Willi Chevalier
Famous for: Competition-winning facial hair
Class: Partial Beard Freestyle
Fact: Rules state that no hair extensions, hair dye or hair pins are allowed.

Stuff Your Face

You should eat three meals a day but American Joey Chestnut seems to have taken this notion a bit too far!

He holds several world records for stuffing his face with food. In 2008, Joey entered the Wing Bowl buffalo-wing eating competition in San Jose, California, USA. He managed to chomp his way through 241 of the sticky meaty morsels in 30 minutes flat to secure his record.

"I didn't grow up wanting to do all this. It's something that chose me."
Joey Chestnut on what drives him to eat for fame

HOT DOG!
Joey also holds the world record for wolfing down the most hot dogs in one go. He managed 66 of the soggy sausages with buns in just 12 minutes.

GUESS WHAT?
A word of warning – eating like this is not recommended unless you have a burning desire to end up the size of a 10-tonne truck!

Stretch Your Skin

While Gary 'Stretch' Turner looks like he is wearing a rubber mask, we can assure you that it's for real.

Gary suffers from a condition called Ehlers-Danlos syndrome that has left his skin incredibly thin and elastic. Able to pull up his neck skin so that it covers his mouth, he enjoys touring the planet shocking and bedazzling audiences worldwide.

●●●●●●●●●●●●●●

So Licky

Sticking your tongue out may be a fun way of passing the time but it's not going to make you famous.

Unless you're Stephen Taylor from Coventry, UK. Measuring a whopping 9.5 cm/3.7 in from lip to tip when sticking out, he holds the official record for the longest tongue in the world. Stephen claims his tongue is still growing and is worried that, one day, it might no longer fit in his mouth!

●●●●●●●●●●●●●●

The Eating Machine

It took two years for incredible Frenchman, Michel Lotito, to eat his way through an aeroplane.

Lotito munched the Cessna 150 aircraft between 1978 and 1980. The stunt brought him worldwide media attention and earned him the nickname Monsieur Mangetout (Mr Eats Everything). His other low-vitamin meals included:

- 18 bicycles
- 7 televisions
- 2 beds
- 1 coffin

GUESS WHAT?

Mr Mangetout died in 2006. Doctors assure us it was of non-metal related causes and his unorthodox diet was not to blame.

STEEL STOMACH

Lotito's ability to munch up to 900 g/32 oz of metal every day was put down to his stomach lining being twice as thick as a normal person's.

"We've tried to understand this phenomenon, these antidotes created by his body, but he's basically just a normal guy."
Dr Bernard Morzol, who studied Mr Mangetout when he was alive

Creepy Cat Man

A pair of fake whiskers wasn't enough for Dennis Enver when he decided to make himself look like a big cat.

Native American, Dennis, had surgery to flatten and upturn his nose, tiger-like fangs inserted into his mouth and covered his body in striped tattoos in a bid to turn himself into a tiger. 'Stalking Cat', as he is now known, is officially the world's most modified man.

BY A WHISKER
Dennis also has had his ears lengthened and attachments fitted to his upper lip so that he can insert proper cat whiskers.

GUESS WHAT?
Mr Cat's Native American upbringing inspired him to take on the appearance of his tiger totem symbol. He began changing his body when he was 23.

STATS 'N' FACTS

Who: Dennis Enver
Famous for: Looking like a tiger
Name: Stalking Tiger
Fact: When not amazing people with his fearsome feline looks, Dennis fixes computers.

"I eat meat every day, just as a tiger would. It must be as close to raw as possible."
Stalking Cat talking to a newspaper

Making A Splash

We all know how painful it can be to belly flop into a swimming pool.

Now imagine what it must be like for Darren Taylor, aka Profesor Splash, from Denver, Colorado, USA, who regularly sets world records for the highest shallow dive. His latest feat was a dive from a height of 10.7 m/35 ft into a mere 30.5 cm/12 in of water!

● ● ● ● ● ● ● ● ● ● ● ● ●

The Big Breakfast

For breakfast, we don't recommend you following in the footsteps of Luppan Yau.

He managed to polish off five and a half breakfasts at the 2007 All You Can Eat Breakfast Eating Championships in London, UK. The greasy brekkies included eggs, bacon, sausages, mushrooms and croissants. Luppan wolfed the whole lot down in an incredible 12 minutes. Indigestion, anyone?

● ● ● ● ● ● ● ● ● ● ● ● ●

PECULIAR PASTIMES

The world is filled with different creeds, colours and cultures. But we're all the same when you get down to it – we all love laughing at our own ridiculousness. So enjoy the freedom over the next few pages and be inspired. Perhaps you will dream up your own peculiar pastime.

Don't forget to check out ...

... the people who dress up as Ninjas in their spare time **p73**

... the man whose hobby is pulling hideous faces **p76**

... and the families that hand their babies over to Sumo wrestlers to make them cry! **p81**

Canonball Superstars

It makes for an interesting discussion around the family dinner table: "Dad, what are you doing today?" Reply: "Well I'm firing myself out of a cannon."

David 'Cannonball' Smith Senior made his name by setting the world record for the furthest human cannonball flight at 76 m/184 ft in 1998. The rest of the family including his sister and his son are following in his footsteps.

BLAST OFF
David still enjoys the odd blast in between making cannons for other family members. He even shot himself over the USA/Mexico border.

GUESS WHAT?
The Smith's act is no walk in the park and requires lots of planning. Once out of the cannon, you must keep your body totally straight at all times.

STATS 'N' FACTS

Who: David Smith Senior
Famous for: Touring the world as a human cannonball
Top speed: 70 mph/112 kmh
Fact: You can expect to experience a g-force of 11 – that's 11 times your body weight.

Air Guitar Hero

Want to experience the thrill of being a guitar hero without actually having to learn to play the guitar? Then this is your moment.

The Air Guitar World Championships are held in Finland each year. Competitors show off their skills to two song snippets – one selected by the organisers and one of their own choosing. Body movement and ludicrous facial expressions are crucial to an amazing performance but no real instruments are ever allowed.

HARD ROCK

You can choose to rock out on imaginary electric guitar or show your sensitive side on acoustic. You may even use a real plectrum for added effect.

GUESS WHAT?

Top tracks selected by the organisers for you to air guitar to include Nirvana's Smells Like Teen Sprit and Green Day's American Idiot.

"It's impossible to be angry and play air guitar."
Zac Monro, Air Guitar World Champion 2001 and 2002

● ● ● ● ● ● ● ● ● ● ● ●

Jets For Thrills

Michel Pont has an expensive but exciting hobby – he collects jet fighter planes.

Since 1985, Michel has owned the biggest private collection of jet fighters in the world. The planes are kept on his 16 hectare/40 acre vineyard in France. But that's not the end of the story. If Michel ever gets bored with his impressive aircraft collection, he can always take a spin in one of his 300 motorbikes or 34 Abarth Fiat racing cars, which he also owns.

STATS 'N' FACTS

Who: Michel Pont
Pastime: Collecting jet fighters
Number in collection: 110
Fact: When Michel isn't admiring his planes, you can find him in his day job as a winemaker.

ON VIEW
If you would like to see Michel Pont's epic collection of planes, motorbikes and cars, they are on view in the museum at his French chateau.

GUESS WHAT?
Michel is unable to take off in any of his planes from his huge vineyard because the fighters are banned from use in French airspace.

Cheesy Run

Every year, crowds gather at Cooper's Hill in the UK to wach crazy folk roll down a hill in pursuit of a lump of cheese in one of the world's maddest events ever.

Totally Crazy

There are five races and for each one, up to 20 people get ready at the top of the notoriously steep hill before the cheese is released. Once rolling, the competitors follow it down the near-vertical slope. Whoever reaches the bottom first is the winner and gets to keep the cheese.

CHEESE WHEEL
A delicious 3.2 kg/7 lb ball of Double Gloucester cheese is used for the event. The circular cheese can reach speeds of up to 112 kmh/70 mph.

"My god! It's not a hill; it's a cliff. People throw themselves down a cliff, after some cheese."
First-time cheese roller, Chris Hodgkins

GUESS WHAT?
Don't think you are safe hanging with the crowd. Both competitors and runaway balls of cheese sometimes roll off into the masses.

STATS 'N' FACTS

Event: Cheese rolling
Where: Goucestershire, UK
How it works: You roll down a slope chasing a ball of cheese.
Fact: Running is allowed but it's safer to slide or roll because the slope is so steep.

Meet the Ninjas

A Ninja festival is held every April in Japan with up to 30,000 spectators – many come dressed for the part.

During the festival, people can be seen clutching maps and walking the streets as they hunt out hidden life-sized Ninja mannequins placed around the city. Families often wear the full gear of the stealth warrior including his 'n' hers matching swords.

STATS 'N' FACTS

Event: Ninja festival
Where: Iga, Japan
How it works: Dress Ninja and celebrate this ancient art.
Fact: It is thought that Ninjas wore dark blue rather than black to hide in the moonlight.

IT'S A SECRET
You can learn more about the Ninja's secret ways in the Igaryu Ninja musuem, which boasts a residence with revolving walls and secret trapdoors.

GUESS WHAT?
Ninjas were prepared at all times. At night, Ninjas would always lie on their left sides to protect their hearts from sudden knife attacks.

In For A Soaking

Fancy a water fight? Then head straight to Thailand between 13–15 April.

Once a year, Thai people take to the streets armed with water pistols, buckets of water and the odd elephant or three to douse residents and tourists alike with sprays of glorious H_2O. This is how the Thai people celebrate Songkran, the official start of the Buddhist New Year.

●●●●●●●●●●●●●●

Canonball Disaster

The Smith family (see page 69) are not the only people who are partial to being shot through the air at ridiculously high speeds. Todd Christian is too.

However, things haven't worked out quite so well for British Todd. Although he doesn't mind being a human cannonball, he has a fear of flying. So when asked to take a long-haul flight to Brazil for a specialist training course, he refused. The result? He was fired from his job – excuse the pun!

●●●●●●●●●●●●●

Big Tomato Splat Fest

It's the world's best food fight and everyone is invited!

To start the fight, which takes place in Buñol, Spain, one person from a vast crowd scrambles up a greasy pole and grabs the leg of ham at the top. Over 40,000 people then start pummelling each other with tomatoes. Known as La Tomatina, the seriously squidgy splat fest takes place every year.

"Never, and we mean never, climb on a gate, window, wall, etc. to be able to watch the battle, you will become the target of 40,000 people."
The golden rule given on the event's website

TOMATO WAR
It's claimed that the first tomato war started in 1945 when a fight broke out between local youths, who grabbed the tomatoes from a market stall.

GUESS WHAT?
Originally, the tomato fight was banned, but in 1955 people marched through the streets with a coffin containing a tomato to get the ban lifted.

Gurn And Bear it

What is gurning and why do people do it? The answer to the former is: the art of pulling faces. The answer to the latter is: who knows?

What we do know is that Briton Tommy 'Quasimodo' Mattinson has won the World Gurning Championships 11 times in a row now and earned himself a righful place in the record books.

"Don't stay like that for too long or your face will stay like that."
Prince Philip to Tommy Mattinson, Gurning World Champion

WRINKLE UP
For the competition, Tommy had to put his head through a horse's collar and scrunch up his face into the most revolting poses imaginable.

STATS 'N' FACTS

Event: Gurning Championship
How it works: You pull the most hideous face you can manage.
Where: Cumbria, UK
Fact: Held at the Egremont Crab Fair, the competition has now become world famous.

Bog Snorkelling

Totally Crazy

It's best not to get too bogged down with this particular preposterous pastime.

The World Bog Snorkelling Championships take place once a year just outside Llanwrtyd, Wales. The premise is simple. Two 55 m/180 ft trenches are dug and contestants are then required to swim down them with flippers and a snorkel, fancy dress hats allowed. Whoever gets to the end first is the winner.

A BIT WHIFFY
The water in the trenches has been described as a pea soup and the smell is bad. Watch out for the odd newt you might swallow as well!

GUESS WHAT?
The sludgy event has been attracting people for over 20 years. People put themselves through the trench warfare in the name of charity.

STATS 'N' FACTS

Event: Bog snorkelling
How it works: You swim through a mud pool with a snorkel.
Where: Llanwrtyd, Wales
Fact: Regular swimming techniques are not encouraged.

Crazy English

The 'Elvis of English' is how Li Yang has been described for his remarkable Crazy English courses.

Chinese Li doesn't give normal classroom-based lessons like a crusty old teacher. No, Li likes to get on stage and teach crowds of 50,000 people at the same time. His technique? To get the audience to shout out the words while pulling an expressive face and gesturing wildly. It really works!

●●●●●●●●●●●●●●

Slippery Pole

Becoming a winner at the annual Independence Day celebrations in Indonesia is a slippery affair.

In the competition, people climb up an oil-coated tree while fellow competitors try to pull them back down to get ahead themselves. Trousers, in particular, are at risk of being lost! But it's all worth it for the prizes at the top of the poles, which may include a bicycle, keys to a brand new motorbike and ... errr ... a plastic bucket.

●●●●●●●●●●●●●●

Wife Wars

Sometimes love can become a drag – quite literally!

Created in Finland, the Wife Carrying Championship started out as a bit of a joke back in 1992 but since then, the craze has swept the planet. The USA, China, the UK, Italy and Australia all enter, with competitors slinging wives over their backs in a 253 m/830 ft assault course.

"The wives and the wife carriers are not afraid of challenges or burdens."
From the Wife Carrying Championship's official website

HEAVE-HO
The challenging course features two obstacles that competitors need to heave themselves over and also a water obstacle which they wade through.

GUESS WHAT?
This race is serious and there are several golden rules including one which says all participants must have fun even if they fall on their faces!

STATS 'N' STUFF

Event: Wife-carrying race
How it works: Men run with a woman flung over their shoulder.
Where: Sonkajärvi, Finland
Fact: One rule is that wives must be over 17 years old.

Incredible Human Tower

Head to Tarragona, Spain, if you ever have the urge to build a human tower.

The famous Castells Competition takes place every two years in the city's bull fighting ring where entrants gather to build the highest human tower. The base is created by a mass of heavy-set people, with smaller groups leaping up to create the next stages. Children are often used at the top because they are light.

•••••••••••••••

Crazy Origami

The amazing Hawaiian Won Park spends his time creating origami figures from the humble US dollar.

Won, the paper-folding expert, has recreated scenes from *Star Wars* and *Star Trek* through to a jumping frog and a toilet with its own lid. He can make just about any object and insists that he never uses glue, sticky tape or scissor cuts of any kind.

•••••••••••••••

Big Cry Baby

At the Crying Sumo competition in Japan, screaming babies are positively encouraged.

Every year, babies born in the area are brought to the Senso-ji temple to compete in a crying contest. Each baby is held by a student sumo wrestler and coaxed into bawling by the students and a temple priest who waves his arms around. If this doesn't work, the wrestlers put on their scary masks. That usually does the trick!

"... Crying Sumo is held to pray for children's healthy growth."
From a report by the Mainichi Daily News

SCREAM LOUD
The competition winner is the baby that bawls first. If both start to howl at the same time, then the loudest screamer takes the trophy.

STATS 'N' FACTS

Event: Crying Sumo competition
How it works: You bring a baby and hope it screams its head off.
Where: Tokyo, Japan
Fact: Sumos are allowed to raise the baby above their heads to encourage howling.

The Vikings Are Back

For one night a year in January, the Scottish bring back the Vikings and run riot through the town.

At the Up Helly Aa festival, you can watch astonishing scenes of grown men dressed in Viking costumes and horned helmets march through the streets of Lerwick, dragging a 9 m/29 ft replica longboat behind them. If that's not impressive enough, they're followed by 900 more people in various disguises carrying fiery torches.

LET IT BURN!
The festival's highlight is the burning of the longboat to music and fireworks, followed by an evening of drinking the Vikings would be proud of!

GUESS WHAT?
Up Helly Aa takes place to celebrate the arrival of the Vikings over 1,000 years ago. The horned ones ruled parts of Scotland for 600 years.

STATS 'N' FACTS

Event: Up Helly Aa Festival
How it works: You dress up as a Viking and drag a boat along.
Where: Shetland Isles, Scotland
Fact: Up Helly Aa is the biggest fire festival in Europe.

Twit Twoo

American Pam Barker got more than she bargained for when she replied to an advertisement for a motley collection of furry and china owls.

In the advert, it stated there were 14,000 pieces of owl memorabilia up for sale but Pam thought this was a mistake and that 1,400 was a more realistic figure. However, it was true and Pam got landed with them all. Let that be a lesson to any collectors out there!

"My husband would like his store back."
Pam Barker on how her collection lives in her partner's building supplies store

GUESS WHAT?
Pam bought her owls after their previous owner died. In tribute, Pam left the previous owner's name in the record books rather than her own.

IT'S A RECORD
Pam holds the biggest collection of owl memorabilia in the world. In total, she has 18,055 feathered friends to dust, wash and keep clean!

WEIRD SPORTS

For some sports, you need to be more than just brilliant – you need to be mad as a hatter as well! So no matter what your shape or size is, you too can become a competition-slaying super sports hero because there is a weird sport out there for just about everybody.

Don't forget to check out ...

... the people who love to race ostriches **p87**

... the chaps who duel with lobsters **p91**

... and the man who invented the crazy sport of extreme ironing! **p99**

Redneck Olympics

Yesiree! Welcome to the Redneck Games, which features the silliest sports in the whole of the USA.

Started in 1996 as a small event to entertain the locals and gently mock the Olympic Games being held up the road in Atlanta, the Redneck Games have become an institution attracting thousands of people. Wacky events include:

• Seeing how far you can throw a hubcap
• Throwing yourself into a rubbish bin to find a prize
• Showing how far you can spit a seed

"All profit – every last cent – from the Redneck Games goes to local charities. We don't make a dime ... That's not what it's about."
Mac Davis, creator of the Redneck Games

BUTT CRACK
You could also enter the butt crack competition! Here people are judged on who has the ugliest butt poking out of the top of their jeans.

GUESS WHAT?
Don't expect to win a gold medal at the Redneck Games. The prize for most events is a trophy with a crushed beer can at the top.

Big Bungee Jump

Why do a bungee jump on your own when you can hang off a cord upside down with 25 others?

This mass jump of mad men and women was performed in 1998 in front of the Deutsche Bank headquarters in Germany. The tightly packed group plummeted 52 m/170 ft before bouncing back up again. It's unofficially the world's biggest mass jump. Let's hope they didn't eat lunch beforehand!

●●●●●●●●●●●●●●

Tweed Run

The next time you're in central London, UK, keep your eyes peeled for a bunch of blokes (well, mainly) on vintage bicycles dressed from head to toe in tweed.

Since 2009, the London single speed and fixed gear cycling forum has welcomed cyclists on a leisurely but stylish jaunt past the capital's finest sites plus a cup of tea in the park. The rules are simple – Harris tweed suits, plus fours and, if you've got it, a penny farthing!

●●●●●●●●●●●●●●

Feathered Speed Fiends

Flightless ostriches might look a bit gangly and useless but these mighty birds can run like the wind.

They're also seriously dangerous and aggressive but that doesn't seem to stop people in some countries from wanting to climb on their backs and race them as fast as they can down a track!

Totally Crazy

"An ostrich that hasn't been worked with can be very cantakerous. They can kill you."
Joe Hedrick, ostrich expert, explains the perils of working with these birds

GET SET, GO!
At Highgate Ostrich Farm in South Africa, ostrich racing is a daily event for the farm workers. Spectators are always kept a safe distance away.

GUESS WHAT?
A rider-less ostrich has a top speed of 64 kmh/ 40 mph. It can outrun a racehorse. A human has absolutely no chance of keeping up.

Swinging On the Wing

Enter the Swing on Wing golfing tournament and you're in for a bit more than gentle shots on the green.

For this crazy competition, held in Abu Dhabi in the United Emirates, you need to balance on the wing of a parked aeroplane and whack the ball with your club as far as you can. Let's just hope driving wind and rain aren't predicted on the day!

● ● ● ● ● ● ● ● ● ● ● ● ●

Donkey Challenge

They may not look like the world's purest thoroughbreds but donkey racing is massively popular.

That includes kids having fun in donkey derbys in the UK, Santas (yes, really!) racing donkeys at festivals in the Swiss Alps and professional jockeys in Germany galloping around a track for prize money. It sounds incredible but one racing donkey was sold for £25,000.

● ● ● ● ● ● ● ● ● ● ● ● ●

Rock, Paper, Scissors ...

While you might think of the game 'rock, paper, scissors' as a way to pass the time, there are others who believe it to be a full-blown sport.

Sean Sears won serious prize money in the Bud Light USA Rock Paper Scissors League Tournament in 2008. But his ultimate challenge was the international championship in China. He managed a respectable bronze, losing out to 'rock, paper, scissors' supremo, Mark Cleland, who took gold.

"Facing off against the finest 'rock, paper, scissors' players in the world was an intense challenge ..."
Mark Cleland, International Rock Paper Scissors champion

YOUR ARSENAL
There is a version of this game that features 22 different objects including guns, lightning, axes, fire, snakes and even nuclear weapons!

STATS 'N' FACTS

Sport: 'Rock, paper, scissors'
How it works: You make weapon shapes with your hand.
Prize money: US $50,000
Fact: The 'sport' is so popular in the USA, it's even televised.

GUESS WHAT?
Some players include dynamite in the game. But there is a dispute that paper could beat dynamite by covering the wick on the stick.

Seriously Mad Soccer

The Brits are bonkers about soccer so this must explain why they play the ever-so-scary Shrovetide soccer match once a year in Ashbourne, Derbyshire.

Known as the 'no rules' game, two teams made up of folk from opposite ends of the town play a match where each team's goalposts are 5 km/3 miles apart. The game boasts hundreds of players and takes two days, with each half of the match lasting a stonking eight hours.

IT'S A GOAL!

To score a goal in this barmy game, you need to hit the ball three times against a specially built plinth which has a mill stone on top of it.

GUESS WHAT?

The game is thought to be 1,000 years old. Some people reckon that it used to be played with a severed head rather than a soccer ball!

STATS 'N' FACTS

Sport: Weird soccer
How it works: Soccer with no rules and as many people as you want on your team.
Fact: There is one rule – you're not allowed to murder anyone!

i Say How Marvellous, Chap

If you're tired of bad manners and oik-ish habits, you could always take part in the Chap Olympics.

Founders, Gustav Temple and Torquil Arbuthnot, who also run *The Chap* magazine, have created a UK-based event to act as a shining beacon to proper behaviour. So once a year, folks turn up in their finest suits and dresses to indulge in silly sports, including:

- Three-trousered limbo
- Pipe smoker's relay race
- Cucumber sandwich, discuss
- Lobster moustache duel

Totally Crazy

STATS 'N' FACTS

Sport: Chap Olympics
How it works: You do silly things politely while dressed in suits.
Fact: Gustav Temple suggests white plimsolls rather than trainers for all events.

SILLY SPORT
Lobster moustache duelling is exactly what it says – two contestants attack each other's moustaches and beards with lobsters. I say!

Armpit Serenade

Are you a master of armpit trumping?

If so, you may want to take a trip to the Redneck Games (see page 85), where this is one of the crazy games. The aim is to create the loudest, boldest trump by cupping your hand under your armpit and flapping your elbow up and down like a mad chicken. If you can play a well-known tune as well, you're guaranteed to win!

●●●●●●●●●●●●●●●

What on Earth is Hornussen?

Good question! Let's start with the basics.

In the Swiss sport of Hornussen, a player thwacks a puck, called a hornuss, mounted on a launcher with a bizarre fishing-rod-style club. The hornuss whizzes through the air at up to 320 kmh/199 mph towards the opposing team. They are holding schindels (wooden placards) and the aim is to catch the flying hornuss without injuring yourself. Get it? No, we don't either!

●●●●●●●●●●●●●●

Get A Mooove On

Forget the elegant sport of horse racing. No, we're more interested in water buffalo racing.

At the heart of the annual water buffalo festival in Chonburi, Thailand, is a buffalo race down a drag strip 100 m/330 ft long. Riders storm down the course, clinging on for dear life without stirrups or saddle, hoping they'll get to the end before the animal decides to do its own thing and not finish, or they fall off.

BUFFALO FIGHT

Some people say that water buffalo racing started because two farmers got into an argument about whose buffalo could run the fastest.

STATS 'N' FACTS

Sport: Water buffalo racing
How it works: You climb on a water buffalo with no saddle.
Where: Chonburi, Thailand
Fact: Some water buffalo are now bred purely for racing.

GUESS WHAT?

In the past, the buffalo also worked the fields for the rice harvest. Locals believed that racing the buffalo made them work quicker.

By George, it's Bounders!

Here's yet another bonkers game from the impeccably dressed contestants at the Chap Olympics (see page 91).

In Bounders, six chaps are given two minutes to behave appallingly to six ladies. Once suitably offended, the ladies must slap the chaps. The cad on the receiving end of the loudest slap is declared the winner. Yes, those chaps really are that mad!

●●●●●●●●●●●●●●

is it A Bird Or A Plane?

No, it's Bognor Birdman actually, one of the many people who attend the seaside town of Bognor Regis in the UK to throw themselves off a pier.

Totally Crazy

Contestants turn up with bizarre flying contraptions to see how far they can get. Many devices are just plain ridiculous like flying hedgehogs or toilets but a few committed engineers arrive with incredible homemade gliders that can travel spectacular distances.

●●●●●●●●●●●●●●

Horse Versus Human

Llanwrtyd Wells in Wales is not only famous for bog snorkelling (see page 77), it is also the starting point for a marathon where humans compete against horses.

You would expect the horses to win every time, but in a surprising turn of events in 2007, two super-fast runners beat the cantering ponies and their riders. The horse camp blamed the overly hot weather for the defeat. What a night-mare!

● ● ● ● ● ● ● ● ● ● ● ● ●

Muddy Belly Flop

Fancy throwing yourself face first into a pit of mud. Well, head off to the Redneck Games (see page 85).

The fatter, the better is the one rule to follow in this seriously sticky event as the contestant's flabby bellies help them to make a big impact in the mud pool. Winners are judged on belly flopping style and the size of the splash they make.

● ● ● ● ● ● ● ● ● ● ● ● ●

Boxing Clever

Chess boxing sees two extemely clever fighters alternating between punching each other and sitting down in the ring for a game of chess.

At the brilliant World Chess Boxing Championships, there are a total of 11 rounds – six rounds of chess and five rounds of fisticuffs. If no one is knocked out or has declared 'checkmate' after all the rounds, the fight is decided on the points earned during the boxing bouts.

HOW UNFAIR!
If there is a tie at the end of the boxing match, the person in control of the black pieces on the chess board is the winner. Hardly skillful!

GUESS WHAT?
The first Chess Boxing Light Heavyweight Championship took place in Berlin in 2007. It was won by German Frank Stoldt, gloves down.

"One minute you're having your skull battered, the next you're sat down trying to work out why you appear to have 48 pawns."
Ringside report, Georgina Turner

Rolling Down the Road

Irish Road bowling is perhaps the cheapest sport known to humans.

This event sees competitors hurling an 0.8 kg/ 1.7 lb iron ball down a closed-off public road. Whoever completes the 4 km/2.5 mile course with the fewest throws is declared the winner. It's hugely popular in Ireland with large crowds gathering. Just watch out that you don't get a huge ball of iron in your face!

●●●●●●●●●●●●●●

Toilet Seat Throwing

Any sport involving toilet seats could only be part of the Redneck Games (see page 85). Here's how it works.

Totally Crazy

Take one lightweight plastic toilet seat and cross your fingers that it's clean. Then throw it carefully, aiming for a stake in the ground. Did we say a stake? We meant a toilet plunger, of course! The person who lands the seat over the plunger handle is the winner.

●●●●●●●●●●●●●●

Get Set ... Glug, Glug

Hearing the firing pistol must have been one of the easier things to do at the Underwater Olympics.

In 2008, Qiando Underwater World in China decided to beat Beijing at its own games by holding a special underwater sporting event. Dressed in wetsuits and laden with scuba gear, divers undertook various events. These included:

• Hurdles in a wet suit
• Fencing with an oxygen tank
• Watery gymnastics

GUESS WHAT?

Not to be outdone, Coex Aquarium in South Korea held their own underwater Olympics. It included underwater soccer and Taekwondo.

TRICKY TARGET

Life was made difficult for divers in the shooting event. They had to stand on a wire while trying to hit an inflated balloon 5 m/16 ft away.

STATS 'N' FACTS

Sport: Underwater Olympics
How it works: Like the normal Olympics but with scuba gear
Where: China, South Korea
Fact: Spectators watch under the water behind a glass wall.

Ironing Man

Totally Crazy

Well, if you're going to iron your pants, why not do it up the side of a mountain?

Created by Phil Shaw, the first Extreme Ironing World Championship for daredevils with a passion for pristine pants took place in Germany in 2002. Competitors had to grab ruffled clothes, irons and ironing boards, then proceed to iron in a series of bizarre locations including up a tree, down a river and while climbing a wall.

"... they forget the main reason they are there in the first place: to rid their clothing of creases and wrinkles ."

Phil Shaw on competitors' obsession with dangerous locations

NOT BORING!
Shaw came up with the idea of extreme ironing when doing the laundry at home. He decided he needed to find a way to make the task less boring.

GUESS WHAT?
The sport of extreme ironing faces some stiff competition from the Urban Housework group who have started up downhill vacuuming!

Cow Dung Golf

Totally Crazy

The Swiss are not normally known for their frivolity but judging from the Cow Dung Golf Tournament, they're starting to let their hair down.

Now in its third successful year, this whiffy sport has competitors marching up the Swiss Alps to see who can hit the most piles of poo with a golf club in two hours. Just imagine the stinky mess at the end!

●●●●●●●●●●●●●●

All Out Wall

It's a barmy sport for posh English people only, so count yourself lucky!

Known as the Eton Wall game, this sport is played only by boys who attend Eton College in the UK. Players are split into two teams and head to a long wall at the school. Then they battle it out, trying to get the ball from one end of the wall to the other by using their feet and piling into one another. It's hardly gentlemanly!

●●●●●●●●●●●●●●

Let's Get Mowing

If you're not rich enough to indulge in Formula One racing, you could always hop on a lawnmower instead.

The British Lawnmower Racing Association boasts four different classes for potential racers, including everything from hand-pushed models to wheel-based mowers that can achieve speeds of up to 80 km/ 50 mph. The event lasts for 12 hours with riders pushing or riding their mowers late into the night.

RACE FOR IT
For the British Lawnmower Racing Association's 25th anniversary in 1997, competitors raced non-stop for 25 hours instead of the usual 12 hours.

STATS 'N' FACTS

Sport: Lawnmower racing
How it works: You find an old or new lawnmower and whizz it round a track as fast as possible.
Where: UK
Fact: The race is an incredible 482 km/300 miles long.

GUESS WHAT?

Fans of lawnmower racing past and present have included the British actor Oliver Reed and motor car racing legend, Sterling Moss.

GROUPS GO CRAZY

They say that people have strength in numbers. Well, judging by this chapter, it simply gives people more of a excuse to behave barking mad. Nothing wrong with that, of course. Perhaps, we should take a leaf out of their books and go a little crazy with our friends once in a while.

Don't forget to check out ...

... the world's largest barbecue **p105**

... and the city where everyone likes to lie down in the snow together! **p109**

Laugh Off Your Troubles

Feeling down? Then take part in World Laughter Day, an event designed to giggle away your blues.

At the heart of all this hilarity is the 'Guru of Giggling', Dr Madan Kataria, who created Laughter Yoga in 1995. It proved so successful that he has now taught people the principles of laughter therapy in over 60 countries, and there are over 6,000 laughter clubs worldwide.

STATS 'N' FACTS

Event: World Laughter Day
How it works: You start laughing and try to infect everyone else.
When: First Sunday in May
Where: Worldwide
Fact: Laughing can bring down your stress and anxiety levels.

GUESS WHAT?

Policemen in Allahbad, India, use laughter therapy at the beginning of their gruelling day to help lift their spirits. You could try too!

HOW TO LAUGH

There is a technique to induce laughter. In a group, start off by faking the laughter. Over time, it will become real because it is so infectious.

Swimming Club

When most people go swimming, they prefer an empty pool with plenty of room to practise their breaststroke.

Not in China, though. They pack themselves in like sardines! Temperatures can get so high in Sichuan province that locals rush to the nearest pool to escape the heat. There's no chance of swimming though. The pools gets so jammed that all you can do is stand there. Let's just hope no one needs the toilet!

● ● ● ● ● ● ● ● ● ● ● ● ●

i Gave My Heart To A Stormtrooper

The 501st Legion is planet Earth's biggest group of organised *Star Wars* fans.

There are over 3,300 members from 30 countries and they like to come together to dress up in stormtrooper costumes. In 2007, 200 members marched down the streets of Pasadena, California, USA, fully kitted out to raise money for charity. George Lucas, the creator of the film series, was in attendance and full of praise.

● ● ● ● ● ● ● ● ● ● ● ● ●

Beef On The Barbie

The people of Paraguay must have eyes bigger than their bellies because they are the record holders of the world's largest one-day open-air barbecue.

Over 30,000 people wolfed down an astonishing 28,000 kg/61,729 lbs of beef in six hours. Alas though, not everyone was happy. Some people complained that there wasn't enough to eat! It seems you can't please all of the people all of the time ...

"It's the largest quantity of meat that has been eaten at one event in one day."
Ralph Hannah, judge at the world's biggest barbecue

NICE NAME
The event's name was 'Todo bicho que camina va al asador'. For you non-linguists, that means 'Every critter walking goes to the barbecue'.

GUESS WHAT?
The world's longest barbecue was pulled off by a group of Russians in 2008. Their spit roasting rack was a staggering 102 m/334 ft long.

Winged Wonders

Flying in formation with just a few skydivers takes skill and practice, so free-falling through the air with 71 people en masse is almost unbelievable.

It took five days of solid practice for the skydiving teams to beat the largest wingsuit formation world record. The team jumped an incredible 30 times over Lake Elsinore, California, USA, before they decided they were ready for an official try. Luckily, they did the job!

"Our biggest concern is a collision in the sky. A collision in the sky would knock you out or break your bones."
Justin Shorb, before the world-record-breaking jump

WHIZZING BY
Four planes were used in the record attempt, each carrying a team of skydivers who hurtled down to the ground at speeds of 161 kmh/100 mph.

GUESS WHAT?
When the skydivers made their amazing jump, there was only 3 m/10 ft separating each one before they opened their parachutes.

STATS 'N' FACTS

Event: Mass skydive
How it works: You jump out of a plane with loads of people while making a shape in the sky.
Where: California, USA
Fact: The skydivers hurtled towards Earth in a V-shape.

Beer Bath

Ever felt like bathing in beer? No, us neither!

However, if the urge does take you, then head off to Hakone spa in Japan. This establishment offers its patrons the chance to submerge themselves in a mug-shaped jacuzzi filled with beer-coloured water scented with hops and barley. Staff pop in three times a day to spray real beer on you – uggh!

●●●●●●●●●●●●●●

Mad About Pants

Totally Crazy

It's not a sight you would normally expect at one of Britain's busiest train stations – a load of people standing around in their underwear.

But that's what travellers to London's St Pancras station were confronted with in 2008. Around 100 shivering people said 'pants to poverty' to promote fairtrade products. The panty-loons made it into the record books for the largest underwear-only gathering!

●●●●●●●●●●●●●●

Jedi Gym Class

Ever fancied a workout with a difference? Well, the Ludosport Lightsaber Combat Academy in Milan, Italy, offers just that.

People are flocking to the Jedi Academy to learn seven different styles of Jedi combat. As well as brushing up on how to brandish a lightsaber without taking your eye out, you also learn how to stop Darth Maul with a throw.

●●●●●●●●●●●●●

Weird Whispers

You'd think that passing a simple message down a line of people might be easy, but it's not so!

A group of British children set a new world record for the longest game of Chinese Whispers. To raise money for charity, 1,330 children gathered in a London football stadium to pass on the message: 'Together we will make a world of difference'. This eventually changed to 'everyone is evil' and by the end over two hours later was just 'haaaaa'. We recommend email in future!

●●●●●●●●●●●●●

City Of Angels

Los Angeles, the city of angels, has been replaced by the city of Bismarck, North Dakota, USA.

In December, 2007, Bismarck's residents turned up to make 8,962 snow angels. To do this, they all threw themselves on their backs at the same time and waved their arms about. It looked extremely silly, but it was a matter of honour, and it gave the city a world record.

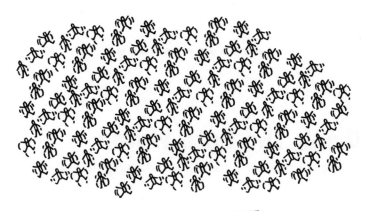

"It's fun and puts us on the map. People think there's nothing going on up here."
Bismarck resident, to the Associated Press

ANGEL BASICS
To make the perfect snow angel, lie in the snow and move as if you're doing a star jump. Then get up and look at the lovely shape you've left behind.

GUESS WHAT?
Everyone got involved. The youngest snow angel was a six-week-old baby and the oldest was 99-year-old Pauline Jaeger.

Leap For Your Country

Want to show your patriotism? Then why not throw yourself out of a plane in the shape of a flag?

That's exactly what 200 Germans did in 2008 to set a new world record for the most Germans free-falling at the same time. With this crazy stunt, they managed to beat the previous record of 156 Germans leaping for their country. Wearing suits in the colours of the German flag, it was truly an impressive sight.

●●●●●●●●●●●●●●

Drink The Bath Water

If your parents are moaning about being stressed, you could recommend the Yunessun Spa in Japan.

In 2009, guests at the resort enjoyed the delights of bathing in a pool filled to the brim with red wine. Staff were on hand to pour glasses of wine for those who couldn't get enough of the booze and were tempted to drink directly from the pool itself!

●●●●●●●●●●●●●

Stiletto Sprint

Some women love their stilettos,
even when they are running in them.

Witness the bizarre site of 265 Australian women racing
each other in Sydney around an 80 m/262 ft course to
break a world record. The winner, Brittney McGlone,
was the first to make it to the end of what must have
been a torturous experience for everyone involved.

"About six girls in front of me fell and two or three heels started spiking up at me."
One competitor, talking to Australia's Daily Telegraph before showing her injury

HEEL RULES
The rules stated that
runners had to wear
7.6 cm/3 in heels. Smooth
legs were also required,
so painful waxing (ask
Mum) was needed.

STATS 'N' FACTS

Event: Stiletto sprinting
How it works: You run as fast as
you can in high heels – ouch!
Where: Sydney, Australia
Fact: A few men were also
spotted in high heels racing.

GUESS WHAT?
Holland held the previous
record for stiletto sprinting.
Only 150 women were
unfortunate enough to
run wearing the
deadly footwear.

Weird Science

Right, here's a 'scientific' experiment for you. Just make sure you do it in the open air with plenty of space around you and your parents on standby!

- Take one large bottle of Diet Coke.
- Now drop one or more Mentos mints into it.
- Keep your head away to avoid a black eye and watch the drink explode out of the bottle in a fizzy fountain.

This trick is all the rage with students in Riga, Latvia. They set off an amazing 1,911 sickly sweet geysers at the same time to bag a world record in 2008.

MINT THEORY
Why does the drink explode? One theory is that the pores in the sweets soak up the carbon dioxide in the Coke, causing the fountain to erupt.

GUESS WHAT?
A rumour says that eating Mentos after drinking Diet Coke can be fatal. No one has died yet, but we suggest you do NOT try to find out!

Strictly Scuba

Seventy-four scuba divers standing at the bottom of a pool sounds like a crowd in need of an open ocean.

But there was a reason for this extreme gathering – they were all taking a dance class while trying to keep in sequence for over 10 minutes. The crazy flipper-footed Australians managed to do just that and set a world record in the process.

● ● ● ● ● ● ● ● ● ● ● ● ●

Gaming Crazy

Zelda, Mario and Sonic are just a few of the popular characters of the videogaming world who all got together in real life in 2008.

A huge group of British fans dressed up as their favourite videogame characters and headed off to the London Games Festival in the UK. There were 342 of the crazy characters, which gave them a world record for the most fans dressed as videogame characters gathered together in one place at the same time.

● ● ● ● ● ● ● ● ● ● ● ●

TOTALLY BIZARRE

It's hard to imagine why some people do what they do. Their ideas and achievements are so wacky that you wonder how they dreamt them up in the first place. So we've rounded up and caged the following out-there madcap items to form this overwhelmingly weird section.

Don't forget to check out ...

... the human lightbulb **p117**

... the woman who lets scorpions crawl over her face **p123**

... and the man who plays the clarinet while covered in bees! **p125**

Freak School

Forget ploughing through the works of Shakespeare. For a truly unique education, enrol at the Coney Island Sideshow School in New York, USA.

Here you can be taught how to be a circus performer in seven days. That means learning the art of sword swallowing, glass walking, fire breathing, escaping from a straitjacket while hanging upside down and how to hammer a spike into your head without dying instantly.

SICK NAME
The teacher who runs the week-long course is the charmingly named Donny Vomit. He's been tossing chainsaws for well over a decade now.

GUESS WHAT?
According to Donny, there are three kinds of freaks: natural, man-made and working. If you learn a skill to perform, that makes you a working freak.

"Be a freak in just one week!"
The Coney Island Sideshow School motto

Peculiar Protestor

If you're a protester and a performance artist, then you've got to do a bit more to stand out from the crowd.

Brit Mark McGowan is just that. Here are a few of his peculiar stunts:

- Sitting in a bath of beans to protest against the negativity surrounding the great British fry-up

- Crawling 88 km/55 miles looking for love with a box of chocolates tied to his body and a rose in his mouth

- 'Sailing' from London to Glasgow in a shopping trolley to improve relations between England and Scotland

"I pushed a monkey nut for seven miles with my nose, from New Cross all the way to 10 Downing Street. I ws protesting against student debt."

Mark McGowan on one of his headline-grabbing protest stunts

SAIL FAILED
Mark's shopping trolley trip ended in disaster after less than a quarter of the journey. He had to give up due to poor weather conditions.

GUESS WHAT?
Mark tried to cartwheel from London to Brighton with rocks strapped to his feet in protest at people taking pebbles from Brighton beach.

Human Lamp

Zhang Deke makes the ideal house guest if you're having trouble with your lights.

Totally Crazy

The 72-year-old highway maintenance man from China likes nothing better than charging his body up with 220 volts of electricity, then placing lightbulbs on his head and ears and lighting them up. Zhang is also able to cook fish on his abdomen in two minutes flat!

GUESS WHAT?

Brit Debbie Wolf says she can make street lights fail when she walks past them. However, scientists are less convinced by her claims.

TESTING TIME

In 1994, Zhang was tested to see how his powers worked. Scientists said he had 'a physical dysfunction' but didn't explain what it was exactly.

STATS 'N' FACTS

Who: Zhang Deke
Famous for: Charging himself up with electricity
Where: Altay City, China
Fact: With his electrical body, Zhang can also help people with ailments such as arthritis.

Toilet Restaurant

The Modern Toilet Diner in Tawain is exactly that – a toilet-themed restaurant.

The seats in the diner are converted toilet bowls and one of the most popular dishes is ice cream in the shape of a dog poo. Now before you start thinking this is just a flash in the toilet pan, you should know there are already 12 restaurants like this in Taipei City, Taiwan.

●●●●●●●●●●●●●●

Squirty Man

Turkish construction worker, Ilker Yimaz, found out he had a special gift while swimming.

No, it wasn't that he could detect pee in the pool, he noticed he could squirt liquid out of his eye. The next step, of course, was to see how far he could squirt it. So in 2004, he wowed the crowds by snorting milk up his nose and shooting it out of his eye in a stream reaching 2.8 m/9.1 ft. His milky antics gave him a world record.

●●●●●●●●●●●●●●

Attack Of The Giant Spiders

If you happened to be in Liverpool, UK, in 2008, you may well have nearly experienced a heart attack after being confronted by a 20-tonne spider.

Constructed from wood and steel, the giant arachnid made its way down the streets of the city. The incredible machine was part of a street theatre production which saw the spider, called La Princesse, causing a spectacle over a five-day period.

"I wouldn't like to meet it in the dark."
Dorothy Wilson, aged 82, to reporters on how she first felt when she saw the colossal spider

STATS 'N' FACTS

Event: Giant marching spider
Created by: La Machine
Height: 15 m/49 ft
Cost: £250,000
Fact: 12 people were strapped into the spider to control her creepy movements.

SQUIRT A LOT
It wasn't a good idea to stand too close to the scary spider. As she crawled along, La Princesse shot a huge spray of water from her abdomen!

Funny Foods

In the West, we like our food 'normal' with a side order of fries. But to people from other continents, our tastes must seem very bland.

If you're driving down the road in Malawi, Africa, you may want to pull over and enjoy the local delicacy of a mouse on a stick. You can buy the dried-out mouse as a fast food snack. Hungry readers will be pleased to know the head, skin and bones are all included in the price.

MOUSE RULES
The proper way to eat a mouse on a stick is by beginning with the tail and working your way up to the head, spitting out the bones as you go!

GUESS WHAT?
In Southeast Asia, Cambodian spider is a delicacy. It's poisonous while alive, but when cooked the critter's venom becomes harmless.

Prison Hotel

Ready to rest your weary head? Then hop on a plane to Germany and visit the Alcatraz Hotel.

This pitstop for tired travellers is a converted prison in the city of Kaiserslautern. You can spend the evening in one of the 57 'cells' available. A genuine prison bed is provided along with traditional stripy convict pyjamas. The windows are, of course, barred.

●●●●●●●●●●●●●●

Bonkers About His Bot

For those looking towards the future, you can do no better than a female android called Aiko.

Scientist Le Trung, who lives in Canada, has created a female robot that can recognise faces, give directions and understand over 13,000 sentences. Trung spends all his time and his savings on his fem-bot. He can be spotted taking her for a spin in the countryside or showing off her skills at technology shows.

●●●●●●●●●●●●●●

Mr Recordbreaker

Most people would be happy to break just one world record in their lifetime, but not Ashrita Furman.

He has set 183 world records in 30 different countries over the past 25 years. Here is a taster of his exploits:

- Balancing a milk bottle on his head while walking for 130.2 km/80.7 miles

- Crushing 53 eggs on his head in 30 seconds

- Somersaulting for over 19 km/12 miles

- Duct taping himself to a wall in 8 minutes and 7 seconds, the fastest time ever

GUESS WHAT?
Ashrita Furman holds one extra special world record - he's the world record holder for holding ... well ... the most world records!

Totally Crazy

"If the stunt won't give you some joy, forget about it. A big part of setting a world record is to have a lot of fun!"
Ashrita Furman offers advice to wannabe world record breakers

Scorpion Queen

Five thousand scorpions, 33 days and a 3 sq m/10 sq ft glass box. Want to know more?

Kanchana Ketkaew deserves her title of scorpion queen after she set a world record in January 2009 for spending the longest time ever confined with poisonous scorpions. The scorpion queen endured being stung by the pincer-wielding horrors 13 times during her record breaking challenge.

STING ME!
Kanchana is able to fight off the ill effects of scorpion poison because she has spent five years exposing herself to their stings in training.

STATS 'N' FACTS

Who: Kanchana Ketkaew
Famous for: Sitting in a boxful of poisonous scorpions
Where: Thailand
Fact: Kanchana was tearful at times during her record attempt but she stuck it out.

GUESS WHAT?
Even though Kanchana's record attempt was hard-going, she has vowed to get back in her box if anyone tries to challenge it.

Underwater Juggler

In 2006, Ashrita Furman, the world's biggest record breaker (see page 122), attempted to beat his own record for the longest time spent juggling underwater.

He set the previous record in New Zealand in 2002 with a time of 48 minutes and 36 seconds. For his second attempt in Malaysia, all was going well until 37 minutes and 45 seconds in, a large shark bumped into him, causing him to drop one of his balls!

●●●●●●●●●●●●●●

Fatal Fish

The Japanese enjoy eating fish, especially if they are poisonous!

The Fugu globefish is a delicacy in Japan even though a deadly toxin can be found throughout its body, including its organs, membranes and even its skin. To be able to eat the fish and actually survive, requires the skill of a specialist licensed chef. It costs up to 20,000 yen (about £150) to enjoy the thrill.

●●●●●●●●●●●●●

Bee-Movie Star

Playing the clarinet covered in bees
is just one of Norman Gary's amazing tricks.

He's also appeared on more than 70 television shows,
done six commercials with bees and set a world record
when he held 109 bees in his closed mouth for 10
seconds while they feasted on a syrup-soaked sponge.

*"Whenever I make a mistake I get stung, so the stings
can be prevented if you're very careful."*
Norman Gary, the bee man

STATS 'N' FACTS

Who: Norman Gary
Famous for: Getting close and
personal with thousands of bees
Fact: Gary looked after the
swarm of bees that featured in
the first *X-files* movie.

GUESS WHAT?

Norman has worked with
bees in films such as the
Oscar-nominated *Fried
Green Tomatoes* and ... err
... *Invasion of the Bee
Girls* in 1973.

Hissing And Kissing

Snake charmer Khum Chaibuddee must be mad – this can be the only explanation for his attempt to break the world record for kissing the most poisonous snakes.

The event occured in October 2006 in front of a Thai audience. They held their collective breaths as king cobras were individually released and then slithered their way onto the stage to be confronted by Khum with his puckered-up lips. Nineteen snakes later and the job was finished, thankfully without incident.

SNAKE SNOG

Khum broke the previous world record for snake snogging, set in 1999 by Gordon Cates. American Cates managed to kiss 11 venomous snakes.

GUESS WHAT?

The king cobra is not the most poisonous snake but it still has so much venom that it can kill an elephant, never mind a human being.

Totally Crazy

STATS 'N' FACTS

Who: Khum Chaibuddee
Famous for: Kissing poisonous snakes one after another
Where: Thailand
Fact: Medics were kept on permanent standby for Khum's snake kissing record attempt.

Snail Bait

One minute you're just a nine-year-old schoolgirl, the next you're setting a gruesome world record.

Tiana Walton is the world record holder for having the most snails sliming their way all over her face – 25 of them, in fact. The rules for setting the record were strict but simple: Tiana had to put as many snails on her face as she could in one minute. Any snails that fell off after a 10 second period were disallowed.

"I am not squeamish. It is relaxing but it feels a bit cold. They are quite smelly and you can see their big long eyes."
Tiana Walton, snail lover

SNAIL COUNT
Tiana's 25 snails beat the previous record of 15 snails. Her mum, Tommy, must be proud. After all, she set the world record for growing the largest lemon!

GUESS WHAT?
Tiana's snail days are now behind her. She really wants to be an Olympic gymnast. Let's hope she can move faster than her slimy chums.

STATS 'N' FACTS

Who: Tiana Walton
Famous for: Letting slimy snails crawl all over her face
No of snails: 25
Fact: After Tiana's world record attempt, the snails were treated to a gourmet meal.

Hospital Food

Visitors to the DS Music Restaurant in Taiwan are in for a shock. You'll never guess from its name that it has a medical theme.

At the restaurant, you are served by waitresses dressed in nurses outfits and receive drinks from IV drips mounted in the ceiling. If that's not enough, the decor includes wheelchairs and crutches, and if you need the toilet, just look for the signs to the Emergency Room.

●●●●●●●●●●●●●●

Performing Pests

Many people think that they are fantasies, but flea circuses, where tiny insects perform incredible feats, actually do exist.

The Floh-Circus, held every year in Munich, Germany, is home to a show where fleas are put through their paces across several disciplines. These include flea soccer and flea-powered chariot races. The dog fleas used weigh less than an ounce and can pull objects that are an astonishing 20,000 times heavier than themselves.

●●●●●●●●●●●●●